EMBRACED

Nurturing Your Child's Identity in God's Unconditional Love

A Teaching Guide to *Puffel* and Introduction to Saint Pope John Paul II's *Theology of the Body*

"In raising children, everything depends on the love relationship between the parent and child. Nothing works well if a child's needs are not met." - Gary Chapman and Ross Campbell

Sr. M. Gianna Casino, LIHM

Foreword by Fr. Augustine J. Wetta, OSB

En Route Books and Media, LLC
Saint Louis, MO

ENROUTE
Make the time

En Route Books and Media, LLC
5705 Rhodes Avenue, St. Louis, MO 63109

Contact us at **contactus@enroutebooksandmedia.com**

Cover design by Siam Pukkato and Sr. M. Gianna Casino

Imprimi Potest: Mother Mary Rose Dorol, LIHM

Imprimatur: In accordance with CIC 827, permission to publish has been granted on November 24, 2025 by Very Reverend Father Carl Scheble, Vicar General, Archdiocese of St. Louis. Permission to publish is an indication that nothing contrary to Church teaching is contained in this particular work. It does not imply any endorsement of the opinions expressed in the publication, or a general endorsement of any author; nor is any liability assumed by this permission.

ISBN-13: 979-8-88870-546-9
Library of Congress Control Number: 2026940812

CONTENTS

Foreword

When it comes to parenting guides, readers are often forced to choose between the practical and the spiritual. In this work, Sr. Mary Gianna has brought the two together with remarkable skill, weaving insights that are at once timeless and contemporary, psychological, and spiritual, educational and recreational.

At its core, *The Catechism of the Catholic Church* provides the theological framework upon which she builds her vision of child-rearing. As a companion to her award-winning children's book, this guide offers the key to unlocking its full richness.

-Fr. Augustine Wetta, O.S.B.

Father Augustine Wetta is a Benedictine monk, teacher, and rugby coach at Saint Louis Abbey in Missouri. He is the author of *Pray. Think. Act.*, *The Eighth Arrow*, and the bestselling *Humility Rules.*

1

EMBRACED BY PARENTHOOD

"Parents have the first responsibility for the education of their children."

CCC 2223

Parenthood begins with a single, profound truth: from the first moment, parents shape their child's life with a love and influence like no other. There are plenty of opinions that swirl around how to raise children, but one cannot deny that parents play a lead role in the life of a child. They are not expected to be experts, but wise stewards entrusted with building a solid foundation for their children to grow upon. With an exclusive insight into their child's world - their dreams, fears, and unspoken needs - parents are called to lead with authentic love, resilience, and accountability.

It's a role that demands sacrifice, from sleepless nights to giving up personal time, and a commitment to model integrity, even when it means owning our mistakes. To be embraced by parenthood is to embrace a calling that is as challenging as it is transformative, shaping not just a child's future but the very essence of who we become.

Parenthood is a vital role, honored by both the Church and society. The Church teaches that parents are the primary educators of their children (CCC 2223), emphasizing that a child's first education begins at home. From the moment a baby is born, they meet their mother, who typically introduces them to their father. Through these earliest interactions, parents lay the foundational pillars of identity and relationship, shaping their child's development from the very start.

In those early years, babies are dependent and consistently manifest their needs. Under responsive parenting, these babies find that their needs are met, especially when hungry, frightened, or distressed. A neurobiological connection is made when a baby is soothed and satisfied (Hughes & Baylin, 2012). This system of positive human interaction is one we learn over time. However, if a baby is consistently ignored, this critical connection falters. Neglected infants may struggle to develop secure attachments, leading to heightened stress responses, impaired emotional regulation, and difficulties forming trusting relationships later in life. Responsive parenting, therefore, is not just an act of love but a cornerstone of a child's lifelong psychological well-being.

From our infancy, our brains are largely molded by others. One of the best things we can experience is the approval, attention, and admiration of people we look up to and love (Perry & Szalavitz, 2017). This gives us a confident sense of self-worth, rooted in the assurance that we are seen and cherished.

Consequently, one of the most painful experiences for a child is when a parent or care-giver fails to appreciate their child's uniqueness. Neglect or belittlement will damage a child. Loss of admiration from those we respect can leave deep wounds. This is why the death of a loved one is also painful. Not being surrounded by love can leave a child confused about their place in the home and in the world.

Planting Seeds of Knowledge and Love

Plants grow and thrive because there are gardeners who know how to take care of them. A plant can receive water, nutrients, and sunlight, but it can still wither. Good gardeners don't just provide water, soil, and sunlight, hoping their seeds will fully grow into plants. Gardeners monitor moisture levels, think of weather conditions, and consider levels of light exposure and shade. They are also vigilant about pests and threats to their plants.

The dignified role of parents as primary educators is a profound calling that shapes the heart, mind, and soul of a child. Just as a gardener carefully tends to their plants with love and vigilance, parents must nurture their children with intention, meeting their needs with responsiveness and fostering an environment where love, identity, and curiosity can flourish.

By being present, modeling good behavior, and offering the approval and admiration that children crave, parents lay a strong foundation for their children to grow into confident, loved, and faith-filled individuals.

Though the journey of parenting is filled with sacrifices and challenges, it is through this selfless love that children come to understand their place in the home, the world, and in God's plan. In this journey, we are called to watch them blossom into the unique and wondrous beings that they were created to be.

Reflection

1. What are ways that you can spend time with your child to foster love, identity, curiosity, and faith?
2. What cherished moments from your own childhood shaped your sense of love and security, and how can you recreate those experiences for your child?
3. Reflecting on your childhood, what challenges or hurts did you face, and how can you protect your child from similar emotional struggles?

2

EMBRACED BY CHILDHOOD WONDER

"The most important period of life is not the age of university studies, but the first one, the period from birth to the age of six. For that is the time when a child's intelligence and curiosity are first awakened, and if we nurture this natural wonder, the child will grow to love learning for a lifetime."

– Maria Montessori

Just like Puffel the Puffin, children are bundles of wonder and curiosity. Children want to know about you, themselves, the world around them, and the world that is to come. They want to know everything. They have a million questions about God. They wonder about Heaven. They want to know why Grandma always has candy in her purse. They want to know why Grandpa falls asleep in the middle of telling a story. Children also have tons of questions about what makes us tick as humans. Like philosophers, children will constantly poke and prod at the universe. And like therapists, they are not satisfied with a half-pint answer. Children will dig deep because they want to understand. Uncomfortable or messy, they want the truth.

As adults who have gone through life, loss, politics, recovery, and redemption, it's up to us to deliver authentic truth. Our children deserve the best!

"He had a colorful beak and a heart full of wonder."

-Puffel

The Inherent Curiosity of a Child

Children's endless questions stem from their curiosity. This should not be discouraged. It helps them to learn. We are naturally curious beings from the moment we are born. This curiosity is already a sign of why God created our minds. To know Him. At a tender young age, the human mind and heart is activated for learning, discovery, and exploration.

To be childlike is to be in awe of God's majesty and creation. This is part of the reason why Christ says, "Truly, I say to you, unless you turn and become like children, you will never enter the kingdom of heaven" (Mt 18:3).

When Plato first founded the Academy, it was an institution of philosophical and scientific inquiry.

The Western school system began with questions, dialogue, and debate. When we allow our children to ask questions, dialogue, and debate in a healthy and moral manner, we are cultivating young minds to learn.

The Role of Play, Imagination, and Discovery

Children love to play, imagine, and discover new things each day. As they grow and interact with you and the people around them, we want them to always remember that they are seen, heard, and loved. This is a crucial stage in their development when they absorb everything. It is the best time to plant seeds of knowledge and love.

Play is the language of children. Children like rules. When they play a game, they instantly ask, "What are the rules?" If children do not have set boundaries or rules to keep them safe, they will not be able to learn and grow.

Child-centered play therapy is also an effective form of child therapy that has proven to be successful with my youngest clients for the same reasons. It builds relationships. The child feels that their actions are important. They know they are seen, valued, and heard. It simply calls for the adult to be truly present as the child is enjoying their play.

Above all, the wonder of childhood is a precious gift. It blends curiosity and delight into understanding the very core of who we are. Just as Puffel the Puffin flutters through life with wide-eyed fascination, our children remind us of the beauty in asking "why," in seeking truth, and in marveling at the mysteries of God and His creation. As stewards of their growth, we are called to nurture this wonder, to meet their questions with patience and authenticity. By embracing their childlike spirit, we not only help them flourish but also rediscover the joy of seeing life through their eyes. A child's spirit also reminds us adults of something important: in every child's heart, we see the truth we long for in life — that we are God's children, deeply loved by Him.

Reflection

1) As you think back to your own childhood, what moments ignited your wonder about life's big questions - about God, Heaven, or the world around you?
2) Who was the person who guided you in exploring those mysteries?
3) How can you guide your child through their challenging questions about faith and life in a way that encourages them to think deeply and grow?

3

EMBRACED BY PUFFEL'S JOY

They [parents] bear witness to this responsibility first by creating a home where tenderness, forgiveness, respect, fidelity, and disinterested service are the rule…Parents have a grave responsibility to give good example to their children.

CCC 2223

Think back to when you were a child. Do you remember having a favorite childhood character or stuffed animal friend? Maybe you've cuddled up with one during a tough night, or perhaps you have watched a child's face light up at the sight of their favorite plush companion. Either way, you are not alone in recognizing the peculiar power that these characters hold in our lives. What is it about them that brings comfort amidst chaos? For a moment, let's step into the world of Puffel - the chilly cliffs of the North Atlantic, where some of the cutest birds on the planet live - the puffins!

What Puffins Teach Us About Life

The main character of the *Puffel* series was created as an Atlantic Puffin because puffins are truly incredible birds. Puffins are great examples of what it takes to create a strong marriage union, build a family, and ensure that their little ones feel deeply loved.

One of the most amazing things about puffins is that they mate for life. Once they find their significant other, they stick with their partners for good. Once in a while, puffins participate in a ritual of "billing." They bond by rubbing their beaks together. Life and love are present in their habitat, making a puffin's home a place of fidelity and tenderness. Although puffins do not possess the free-will and complex intelligence of human beings, they thrive at faithfulness to one another naturally. If puffins are capable of this fidelity, then we are capable of being faithful as well. Commitment comes on a natural level, but we need grace to sustain it and to flourish in our relationships.

Puffins also carry the role of a family. Atlantic Puffin birds are known for being responsible, having large colonies, and caring for their young. A puffin couple has one puffling per year. Each year, they return to the same burrow. What is even more inspiring, is how a mother puffin and father puffin share parenting duties. A little puffling's appetite is insatiable. In one day, a parent may dive up to 276 times, and hold up to 10 fish in its beak each time to feed its puffling. Puffins must constantly make sure their child is supplied with fish. The puffling swallows the fish headfirst and whole. By the time the puffling leaves its burrow, each parent will have dove 12,420 times.

It is the parent puffin's natural instinct to bond with their child and work hard for them. So, the next time you see a picture of these adorable birds with their colorful beaks and funny walk, remember how hard they work to take care of their little ones.

Puffins are remarkably social creatures, thriving in vibrant, bustling colonies during the breeding season. While puffin parents venture out to sea to gather fish, their little pufflings remain in the colony, engaging in lively interactions with their peers. These young birds squawk, waddle, and play together, forming bonds as they eagerly await their parents' return with nourishing treats. This natural sociability in puffins offers a valuable lesson for parents: fostering social connections is essential for a child's growth. Beyond nurturing family bonds, we aspire to raise children who are kind, courteous, and well-liked, capable of building meaningful friendships.

In Puffel's story, we see this from the beginning when Puffel eagerly rushes to join his friends, excited by the snow-covered ground. In the sequel *Puffin Meets a Narwhal*, the narrative deepens this theme, highlighting friendship and community as cornerstones of a child's emotional and holistic development. For many children, shyness can be a hurdle, making it vital for parents to gently encourage playtime and interactions with others. By creating opportunities for socialization, we help our children develop confidence, em-pathy, and the skills needed to forge lasting relationships, much like the spirited pufflings in their lively colonies.

Puffin Parenting

In the story *Puffel,* Puffel begins to compare himself with the penguins. This is also when he begins to doubt himself. When Puffel's feelings become a concern, we see Mama Puffin and Papa Puffin speak with Puffel separately because each parent has something unique to offer. Each parent makes quality time with Puffel, just as puffins in the wild, will take turns being with their child. When Puffel is sad, Mama Puffin wraps her wings around him and asks what troubles him. She later teaches Puffel about the gift of who he is. Papa Puffin also confronts Puffel and sits Puffel on his lap, explaining the neatness of the variety of birds in the world when he sees his son struggling. Similarly, you will find your own way of doing things with your child's best interest at heart.

You may also find that your parenting style

may be different from your spouse's parenting style. One parent may appear to be firmer and more serious at times, and the other parent may appear more fun or gentle. Your parenting style could also be a blend of several styles. However, you are both ordained with authority. There are no perfect parenting styles. However different the style is, your child needs you both to be present.

When times get tough, Christ offers us a Perfect Father and a Perfect Mother to turn to. God the Father is the Perfect Father. The Blessed Virgin Mary is the Perfect Mother. Teach your child to love them always.

Reflection

1) How do you display affection to your children? You say you love them, but do they *feel* that you love them? What do you do to show this? Ask your child:

   What makes you feel happy when we spend time together?

   What's your favorite thing we do that shows I care about you?

2) What is your parenting style? Is it based on love? Is it at times driven by fear, denial, or negative emotions?
3) Do your children witness bonding moments between you and your spouse? If there is an argument in front of them, do you apologize in front of them as well?
4) How often do you invite company and family friends into your home or arrange plans to meet with them? Does your child see how you respectfully interact with other family members and adults in a healthy, whole-hearted manner?

4

EMBRACED BY LIFE'S PURPOSE

"My favorite illustration in the book is when Mama Puffin is hugging her son. Every parent should be like a warm blanket for their child."

-Nadya Izotova, Illustrator of Puffel

Puffel is a story that delves into how love reveals our true identity. Love connects us all and serves as the foundation of our existence, for God is love (1 Jn 4:8). Since we were made in the image of God, we were made in the image of love. To love is a means and an end. It is both natural and supernatural. Early on, children can understand that they were made by love, in love, and with a purpose to love.

Capacity to Love

As children, we are shaped by others who teach us about life's meaning and purpose. Through our experience with those people, we also learn about love. Children crave a sense of belonging and have an innate ability to love others deeply. This capacity for connection and relationship is at the core of what it means to be human. In essence, we are called to love God and love our neighbor without reservation. Christ tells us this when He says, "As I have loved you, so you also should love one another" (John 13:34). Children have the wisdom to easily grasp this concept.

Loving Children

There is a special love children must feel. Unconditional love. It is a love that is not based on what a child does, but based on who the child is. It is a love that accepts and affirms the child, even in failure. Showing love takes effort and sacrifice, as Mother Teresa says: "Love cannot remain by itself - it has no meaning. Love has to be put into action and that action is service."

Genuine, unconditional love is the most beautiful thing in the world that a child can feel. As St. John Bosco once emphasized, telling a child they are loved is

not enough, they must feel it in their hearts. When a child feels loved, they can thrive in learning, discipline, and other aspects of life. This special love is not based on performance but on accepting and affirming the child for who they are, even when they make mistakes. Mistakes and failures should be acknowledged. Wrong decisions, poor choice of words, and disrespect should not be excused, but they should not displace a parent's expression of love to a child. After all, good discipline and correction of behavior comes from a loving place. We discipline because we want our children to live virtuously.

Setting expectations is necessary, but a child not living up to them does not justify withdrawing love. When expressing love to your child is contingent upon their performance, it fosters love that is conditional.

This leads a child to low self-esteem and anxiety, regardless of if they are performing well or not (Assor & Tal, 2012). Children may begin to tie their self-worth to external measures like grades, appearance, popularity, or adult approval. As they navigate their teenage years, exposure to peer pressure and social media amplifies these risks. Those inclined toward people-pleasing or seeking validation may be particularly vulnerable to pursuing approval from unhealthy sources.

This is why validation from you is so important. If they lack admiration and respect from the people who are closest to them, they will perceive that they are simply "not good enough." It pains a child to think that he or she will "never be good enough" for Mom or Dad, relatives, or teachers. Whether your child is an infant or young adult, your child needs to hear and feel your love, simply because they exist. The search for external validation will leave them unfulfilled when it doesn't satisfy their inner longing of acceptance.

Identity

Take time to imagine the most beautiful place you have ever seen on earth. Imagine what you see and hear. At first sight, it is breathtaking. You have never seen anything like it. Upon this sight, you are in awe of such beauty. Have you ever thought that this is the way that God the Father sees us? Can we imagine that when God sees us in His image, He marvels at our beauty? Who we really are, is who we are in the eyes of God. Known. Beloved.

Now imagine a child wrapped in the loving embrace of a parent, smiling and safe. The child sees a look of adoration and unconditional love in the parent's eyes, mirroring the love of God. In this sweet moment, there is a mixed scent of baby shampoo and innocence. No sound but silence. Where there is true love, words aren't necessary. A father's embrace feels like a shield, protecting us from harm. God's touch is gentle yet firm, always guiding us on the right path and reassuring us of His constant presence. Children are more than deserving of knowing what this love feels like, a love modeled after God's Divine Fatherhood.

Affirming a Child's Identity

Akin to the loving embrace of God, we can sense our true identity as beloved, in the gentle touch of a parent's hand on our shoulder, assuring us that we are loved and valued. One of the most significant ways to positively influence your child is by nurturing their sense of self through spending time with them, praying with them, having meaningful conversations, setting a good example, offering praise and showing affection.

What does parental affection look like? Affection is gentle, kind, and tender. Make your child get used to it. There is plenty of teasing and roughhousing in society that show affection between friends and siblings. In our day and age, the world needs tenderness.

The warmth of a hug, the gentle stroking of a hand through a child's hair, the softness of a kiss on their forehead. These actions speak love and comfort, reminding the child of their worth and identity in the eyes of God. Parents are the ones who count their baby's toes over and over again. It is their duty to have a shoulder to cry on when their child scrapes their knee for the first time riding a bike. These are the pleasures and joys of parenting. By modeling unconditional love, we raise children to become life givers.

Children also enjoy giving this kind of love as much as they enjoy receiving it.

Sometimes parents may compare their children to other children, in hopes that their child will change their behavior. Does this motivate a child towards embracing their identity? Does comparison to other people, ultimately move them towards goodness? Or is this teaching them to compare themselves to others? Does comparison truly motivate a child to do their best? Instead of behavioral change, the child learns to compare.

To motivate a child, our actions must be ones of encouragement and affirmation. If you want to correct or discipline a child, your love must be rooted in clarity and consistency in consequence. These healthy actions guide them toward understanding. Not fear or low self-worth.

Affirming a child's identity through loving, tender actions like hugs, gentle touch, and meaningful time spent together fosters a deep sense of self-worth and belonging, reflecting the unconditional love of God. By prioritizing affection over comparison, parents can nurture their children into becoming compassionate citizens of God's Kingdom. They will value themselves and others, rather than becoming caught in a cycle of self-comparison. This approach not only strengthens a child's identity but also equips them to navigate the world with confidence and kindness, embodying the love they've received.

Purpose

When teaching the purpose of life, children should know that they were created to know God, to love God, to serve God, and to be with Him forever in Heaven. Children have a great capacity to love others deeply with pure hearts, just as they have the capacity to know and love God above all. Engage your child in a simple conversation: Ask, "Why do you think God gave us our minds?" Gently answer, "To know Him." Then ask, "Why do you think He gave us our hearts?" Respond, "To love Him."

Reflection

1) God the Father sees you with infinite love and knows you completely. When you imagine how God looks at you, what do you feel or see in His gaze?
2) How can knowing that you were made to love and serve God shape the way you treat others in your daily life, especially your children?

5

EMBRACED BY GOD'S GIFTS

"The ultimate gift is to make a child feel invited to exist in our presence exactly as he is, to express our delight in his very being."

- Gabor Maté, M.D., Gordon Neufeld, Ph.D

Gift-giving is a love language. Knowing what we have been given is essential when we reflect on our purpose and meaning in life. Through knowing his gifts, Puffel understands how loved he is. In this chapter, we explore the divine gifts God bestows upon us. Family, the body, masculinity and femininity, and the virtues that shape our hearts. These gifts, given freely by our Heavenly Father, anchor us in His love and guide us toward our true identity as His beloved children. In Puffel's story, Puffel's gifts help him embrace who he is, even when his outer world tempts him to wish he were something else.

The Gift of Family

Among the first gifts we receive in life is family. When considering a person's identity, it is nearly impossible to separate them from the profound influence of their family.

The family is a holy image that reflects God's love, mirroring the communion of persons in the Holy Trinity. The Catechism of the Catholic Church (CCC) states, "The Trinity is a mystery of faith in the strict sense, one of the 'mysteries that are hidden in God"(234).

Within this mystery, the Father is the source of love, the Son is the beloved who receives and returns that love, and the Holy Spirit is the bond of love proceeding from their mutual self-giving. This dynamic of love within the Trinity serves as the archetype for all relationships, especially the family. The family, as a community of persons, is called to reflect this divine communion through mutual love, self-gift, and fruitfulness.

The Church teaches that "the family is a kind of 'school of deeper humanity,' love, and hope for society" (Vatican II, "Gaudium et Spes," #52). We see this connection in the genealogy of Jesus in Matthew 1:1-17. His lineage is traced from Abraham through David to Joseph, the foster father of Jesus. In this lineage, we also learn about people like Rahab and Ruth. Their stories show how family shapes identity and fulfills God's covenant in reflecting His unconditional love for all humanity.

Just as the Trinity exists in unity and love, the family, despite its imperfections, ought to serve as a space where God's grace nurtures identity, love, and hope.

The Catechism of the Catholic Church teaches:

> *"The family is the original cell of social life. It is the natural society in which husband and wife are called to give themselves in love and in the gift of life. Authority, stability, and a life of relationships within the family constitute the foundations for freedom, security, and fraternity within society. The family is the community in which, from childhood, one can learn moral values, begin to honor God, and make good use of freedom. Family life is an initiation into life in society" (2207).*

When you think about your child, consider what they see when they look at your family. Do they find a true home - a place of safety, love, and belonging? Your family is more than just a household; it's the first place where your child learns who they are, how to love others, and how to know God. As the original cell of society, your family shapes your child's understanding of themselves, their moral values, and their faith.

Imagine that this is the place where your child discovers their identity as God's beloved. For this reason, the family is also known as the domestic church. In this space of communion, a child first learns to pray, love God, and live with faith, hope, and charity.

Puffel's story shows what it means to find comfort and faith in the home. Atlantic Puffin birds, are known for their lifelong fidelity, thriving in large, supportive colonies, and tenderly caring for their young. In the *Puffel* series, Puffel's family surrounds him with encouragement. When Puffel doubts himself, Papa Puffin and Mama Puffin remind him of his unique place in their family and in God's creation. In a similar way, children can be taught to pray, to trust in God's love, and to see themselves with compassion. Through the love of his parents, Puffel learns that he is enough, just as he is.

The Gift of the Body

God gave Adam stewardship over His creation and the animals. As Adam cared for the animals and observed them, he realized his body was distinct from them. Similarly, in our story, Puffel encounters penguins during playtime and notices how different he is from them. Puffel sees that his short wings and colorful beak contrast with the penguins' sleek bodies and black-and-white feathers. At first, Puffel feels "limited" compared to the penguins, who glide so gracefully through the water. But then, Papa Puffin gently explains that Puffel's body is perfectly designed for his purpose - to dive deep, soar above the waves, and build a home in the cliffs.

Puffel learns that his body is a gift, uniquely crafted by God. Just as puffins have abilities that penguins do not have, humans are set apart as created in God's image and likeness (Gen 1:27). Only humans can reason, choose freely, and love with a heart open to God. Our bodies are temples of the Holy Spirit. They are holy vessels of God's presence. The body also reflects God's design in two distinct ways: male and female. Each has unique gifts. Women, for example, have the extraordinary capacity to nurture and give life. We live in a world where children will encounter conflicting ideas about the body from different voices. Parents must guide them to cherish this profound truth: you are a body and a soul, fearfully and wonderfully made (Ps 139:14).

Try this with your child: Ask simple questions to help them reflect on their body and soul. "When you're hungry, is that your body or soul talking? When you feel sad about something that happened, is that your body or soul?"

These questions spark wonder and help children see themselves as God sees them - whole, loved, and purposeful.

The Gift of Masculinity and Femininity

Helping children understand masculinity and femininity is based upon knowing that God created them to reflect His love and purpose. Puffel finds joy in discovering his purpose and unique gifts.

The human person is a being of extraordinary dignity. We are created not only to reflect God's goodness and beauty, as all creation does - but even more. To bear His very "image and likeness."

While creation and creatures glorify God through the gifts they've been given, humans have the privilege of actually contributing to God's glory through their understanding and freedom to love (Fredoryka, 2010). Every child expresses this dignity to love through virtue, which requires understanding and freedom. The kindness to help another person, the compassion to nurture, or the courage to face adversity, are examples of numerous ways which reveal God's design for humanity - to ultimately love.

To anchor this understanding, parents can share the story of Genesis 1 which teaches that God created humans as male and female, both in His image. This part of Sacred Scripture shows children that being male or female is a fundamental part of being human, each reflecting God's love and glory in unique yet equal ways.

> *Then God said: Let us make human beings in our image, after our likeness. Let them have dominion over the fish of the sea, the birds of the air, the wild animals, and all the creatures that crawl on the ground. God created mankind in his image; in the image of God he created them; male and female he created them.* Genesis 1:26-27

Parents play a vital role by celebrating their child's God-given identity and encouraging them to embrace their masculinity or femininity as a gift, not a limitation. This means fostering an environment where children feel free to explore their talents and callings without being confined by stereotypes. Sometimes cultural expectations demand that boys be "tough and aggressive" or girls "must be delicate." Too much focus on norms or physique can diminish the richness of the human person. To fully grasp what it means to be male or female, children must first recognize the profound dignity of the human person. Above all, this is knowing that they are created to love, create, and live in relationship with God and others. By focusing on this inherent worth, parents can help children see masculinity and femininity as harmonious expressions of God's plan, not as opposing or limiting roles.

In Puffel's story, Mama Puffin and Papa Puffin embody this gift of teaching values through their teamwork and love. When Puffel is distressed over the things he can't do as a puffin, each parent takes a different approach in addressing this. Papa Puffin's strength lies in giving Puffel a broad sense of the kind of bird he is (reading Beakipedia to him) and also providing for him (as he works). Mama Puffin shows her nurturing care as she gently rubs his beak and tells Puffel how perfectly lovable he is. Together, Mama and Papa reflect the unity and diversity of God's love. Puffel sees in his parents a model of how masculinity and femininity work in harmony, each bringing unique gifts to their family.

Three Gifts of Theology of the Body

As parents, you want your children to know who they are in God's eyes - beloved, unique, and created for love. Pope St. John Paul II's Theology of the Body offers profound insights into human identity through three foundational "gifts" revealed in the Book of Genesis: Original Solitude, Original Unity, and Original Nakedness. These gifts help us understand our children's identity. They invite all of us to see ourselves and others with God's loving gaze. To make these truths come alive, we'll explore each gift through the playful stories of Puffel - a character whose adventures mirror these theological realities in ways children and parents can both grasp.

The Gift of Original Solitude: Discovering "Who Am I?"

In the beginning, God created Adam – the first human being. He created Adam alone - not to leave him lonely, but to help him discover who he was in relation to God and the world. Original Solitude is about recognizing our unique identity as individuals made in God's image. When Adam named the animals (Genesis 2:19-20), he realized that he was different. He was not just another creature, but a person with a body and soul, capable of thinking, choosing, and loving. He was part of creation yet set apart, aware of his special relationship with God. This solitude is not loneliness. It's the space where we ask, "Who am I? Why am I here?" and find answers in God's love.

In the first story, Puffel is a young puffin who discovers his unique gifts of flying speedily and diving deeply. When his family and friends affirm these talents, Puffel begins to understand his individuality. Penguins can't fly at all. Like Adam naming the animals, Puffel sees his place in the world - not just as one among many, but as a unique being with a purpose. His story reflects Original Solitude by showing children that they, too, are special, created by God with gifts that set them apart. Parents can use Puffel's journey to encourage their children to explore their own talents and to seek God's voice in discovering who they are meant to be.

Reflection

What are your child's unique gifts? Help them to recognize those gifts, just as Puffel's loved ones affirmed his. Consider asking:

1) What makes your heart happy?
2) What's your favorite thing to do that makes you smile big?

Use Playful or Visual Prompts: Incorporate activities to make the question more accessible:

- **Drawing**: Can you draw something you love doing that makes you super happy?
- **Storytelling**: If we made up a story about you having the best day ever, what would you be doing?
- **Puppets/Toys**: Use a stuffed animal to ask, What does Mr. Bear love to do? What do *you* love to do?

Observe Nonverbal Cues: Young children may express themselves better through actions or expressions than words. Watch their body language or excitement when they talk about certain activities.

Point out their unique qualities. "God gave you a very caring heart – that is so special!" Point them to God as their loving Father and the source of their identity.

The Gift of Original Unity: Finding Joy in Communion with Others

Original Solitude leads to Original Unity, the gift of being created for relationship. When God saw that it was "not good for the man to be alone" (Genesis 2:18), He created Eve. Adam exclaimed, "This at last is bone of my bones and flesh of my flesh" (Genesis 2:23). When Adam formed a bond with Eve, he finally felt whole and even felt like a new man. God ordained this union from the beginning. Together, man and woman reflect God's image through their communion. It is a mutual gift of self that brings joy and wholeness. Original Unity teaches us that we find ourselves not in isolation but in giving ourselves to others in love.

In *Puffel Meets a Narwhal*, Puffel encounters Nizzle, a narwhal who becomes his friend. Through their friendship, Puffel experiences a special joy in Nizzle's presence, discovering the goodness of another being. This mirrors the joy Adam felt when he met Eve, finding someone who complemented him. Puffel and Nizzle's friendship shows children that relationships - with friends, family, or community - are essentially a gift from God. Their story illustrates how we are made to share life with others. We are meant to find completeness in mutual love and support.

Encourage your child to build friendships like Puffel and Nizzle's, ones where they can share their gifts and celebrate others' gifts. Teach them that true friendship involves giving and receiving love, reflecting God's design for unity.

Ask Your Child

1) Can you tell me the name of one person in your class? What are they like?
2) What is your favorite thing to do during your free time at school? Is there a class-mate that enjoys that same activity?
3) Today, can you ask one person in your class what their favorite color is and tell us at dinner time what you found out?
4) Who are your friends?

The Gift of Original Nakedness: Seeing with God's Eyes

Original Nakedness is the gift of seeing ourselves and others as God sees us - beautiful, good, and created for love. In Genesis, Adam and Eve were "both naked, yet they felt no shame" (Genesis 2:25) because they saw each other with pure hearts, beholding not just bodies but souls. They saw the other's goodness and their call to love, free from fear or selfishness. This gift reminds us that our bodies are not objects to be used. Our bodies are signs of God's love. They reveal our dignity and purpose.

In the story *Puffel's Masterpiece*, Puffel faces a terrifying event wherein a prized possession breaks into pieces. Yet, from this brokenness, something even more beautiful emerges. This story reflects Original Nakedness by showing that even in our vulnerabilities, God sees us as His masterpiece. Puffel's journey teaches children that their worth isn't diminished by mistakes or hardships. Instead, God can transform brokenness into beauty, just as He sees us with love despite our flaws.

Puffel's stories offer a playful yet profound way to share the Theology of the Body with your children. Through Original Solitude, they learn they are unique and loved by God. Through Original Unity, they discover the joy of relationships. Through Original Nakedness, they see their worth and the beauty God creates, even in brokenness. As parents, you can guide your children to embrace these gifts, helping them grow in God's fatherly love as His beloved sons and daughters.

Reflection

Help your child see themselves and others through God's eyes, as Puffel learns to see beauty in brokenness. When they face challenges, remind them that God loves them unconditionally and can make all things new.

Ask: "How can we find something good even in tough moments?"

6

EMBRACING BIG VALUES FOR LITTLE HEARTS

"Anyone who does anything to help a child in his life is a hero to me."

-Fred Rogers

The home is the ideal place to nurture virtues. Virtues are the building blocks of a life rooted in God's love. The Catechism reminds us: "The home is well suited for education in the virtues. This requires an apprenticeship in self-denial, sound judgment, and self-mastery - the preconditions of all true freedom" (CCC 2223). Through Puffel's journey, we explore five key virtues that help children grow in God's love: self-compassion, self-acceptance, gratitude, empathy, and friendship.

Addressing Values and Challenging Topics: Your Role as a Parent

Papa Puffin and Mama Puffin act as a team when addressing important topics with their child. Parents are the first teachers in their children's lives, and children learn through the love modeled in the home. It's essential to communicate openly with your child about virtue, identity, masculinity, femininity, and how to respond to opposing views. Communication builds trust and equips children to navigate challenges with confidence in God's truth.

In the story, Puffel faces a difficult moment when he declares he'd rather be a penguin than a puffin. Mama Puffin responds with empathy.

"She understood him." She listens to Puffel's heart without judgment. Yet, she also knows the true beauty of being a puffin. She gently reminds him of his unique gifts - his ability to fly, dive, and build a home in the cliffs. Papa Puffin also helps Puffel when they read a bird encyclopedia together. Puffel sees the beauty of different kinds of birds. Together, Puffel's parents help Puffel see that his identity as a puffin is a gift, not a flaw.

When challenging moments arise, parents can follow this model: listen with empathy, affirm your child's feelings, and guide them toward truth with love. The best gift is to assure a child that they belong, exactly as they are, and to express our joy in simply being with them. (Neufeld & Maté, 2019). This builds a foundation of trust, allowing children to face the world with courage and self-acceptance.

Self-Compassion

Self-compassion is rooted in humility. It is the gentle acceptance of ourselves without judgment. Even more, it is us extending compassion to ourselves when we make mistakes. Children are naturally good at this. They make mistakes, get corrected, and get back up again.

There will be things that children like about themselves and things they like about their family. There will also be things that they may not like so much. When Puffel feels discouraged about his differences from the penguins, Mama Puffin teaches him to be kind to himself. She reminds him that God created him to be a puffin for a reason, and his worth doesn't depend on being like anyone else. Parents can model self-compassion by showing children how to approach themselves gently with the same love God has for them. They are perfectly lovable in their existence.

Self-Acceptance

Self-acceptance is the ability to embrace oneself fully, recognizing and appreciating one's unique qualities, strengths, and imperfections. For parents, nurturing self-acceptance in their children is a vital part of raising confident, resilient individuals. However, the desire to see their children achieve greatness can sometimes lead parents to set unrealistically high expectations. While these expectations may be well-intentioned, they can inadvertently cause children to become overly critical of themselves, fear failure, or hesitate to ask for help when needed.

Puffel's parents model a balanced approach to fostering self-acceptance. They celebrate Puffel's unique puffin traits: his colorful beak, his quirky waddle, and his love for diving and flying across the sea. They celebrate uniqueness even when Puffel doubts himself. Instead of pushing him to conform to external standards or comparing him to others, they affirm his inherent worth and encourage him to trust in God's design for his life. This approach helps Puffel develop a sense of security and confidence. This strong sense helps children to be confident when facing challenges and societal pressures to be something they are not.

Parents can cultivate self-compassion and self-acceptance in their children through intentional, faith-centered practices:

- **Praise Effort Over Perfection**: Acknowledge your child's hard work and progress, regardless of the outcome. This teaches them that their value lies in their effort and character, not just their achievements.

- **Affirm Inherent Worth**: Remind your child that they are loved and valued for who they are, not for what they do. Ground this affirmation in the belief that they are wonderfully made by God, with unique gifts and purposes.
- **Encourage Seeking Guidance**: Teach your child to turn to God, the Blessed Mother, St. Joseph, the angels and saints in moments of doubt or struggle. By modeling prayer and trust in divine guidance, parents can help children find peace in their identity and direction in their challenges.
- **Create a Safe Space for Mistakes**: Allow your child to fail without fear of judgment. Use mistakes as opportunities for growth, reinforcing that setbacks are a natural part of learning and development.

By fostering self-acceptance, parents empower their children to embrace their God-given uniqueness, navigate life's challenges with confidence, and resist the pressure to conform to unrealistic standards. Like Puffel's parents, celebrating a child's individuality and grounding him or her in faith can lay the foundation for a life of self-assurance and purpose.

Gratitude

Gratitude transforms our perspective. It helps us focus on what we do have rather than what we lack. When Puffel envies the penguins' abilities, Papa Puffin shows Puffel that each kind of bird has unique qualities. Together, they look at parrots, toucans, chickens and more in his encyclopedia of birds, *Beakipedia.* Puffel becomes grateful for his colorful beak, his strong wings, and his loving family. By practicing gratitude, Puffel learns to see his life as a gift by God's design. Parents can cultivate gratitude in their children by sharing daily moments of thankfulness, such as praying together at meals or naming three things they're grateful for each day.

Empathy

Empathy is the ability to understand and share another's feelings. Even a little empathy goes a long way and reflects God's compassionate heart. Mama Puffin models empathy when she listens to Puffel's struggles without judgment. She enters his world, helping him feel seen and loved. Parents can teach empathy by encouraging children to notice others' feelings, pray for those in need, and act with kindness. Simple questions like, "How do you think your friend felt when that happened?" can nurture a child's empathetic heart. Letting them know that life circumstances can deeply affect us is incredibly important.

Friendship

Man is not meant to be alone. Friendship is a gift that helps us thrive and grow closer to God. In Mere Friendship, C.S. Lewis writes, "We are unfashioned creatures, but half made up, if one wiser, better, dearer than ourselves - such a friend ought to be - do not lend his aid to perfectionate our weak and faulty natures." Lewis understands friendship to be a spiritual relationship in which another person helps us grow toward our full potential. St. Thomas Aquinas adds, "There is nothing on this earth more to be prized than true friendship." Puffel is a very social bird who has plenty of puffin friends, but in the second story, we see him grow in wisdom when he meets Nizzle the Narwhal. This friendship helps Puffel see his gifts through another's eyes, reinforcing his identity as a beloved puffin. At the same time, Puffel realizes that empathy is key to understanding others and making new friends. Parents can encourage friendship by teaching children how to be respectful and courteous with others. They can also encourage them to spend time with others who share their values and lift them up in faith.

God's gifts are endless. Among them are the family, the body, masculinity and femininity, and virtues like compassion, gratitude, empathy, and friendship. All are invitations to know His fatherly love. Through Puffel's story, we see how these gifts guide a child to embrace their true identity. As parents, you are called to nurture these gifts in your children, helping them shine as God's beloved.

Reflection

1. How can you model self-compassion and self-acceptance in your own life to inspire your child? What is one way you can show delight in your child's unique identity this week?
2. Puffel learned to be thankful for his puffin gifts. Ask children: What is one thing you're thankful for about the way God made you?
3. How does your family act like a "domestic church"? What is one new way you can pray or show love together consistently?

7

EMBRACING SAINTLY WISDOM

"When we had our children, our ideas changed somewhat. We lived only for them. They were all our happiness, and we never found any except in them. In short, nothing was too difficult, and the world was no longer a burden to us. For me, our children were a great compensation, so I wanted to have a lot of them in order to raise them for Heaven."

-St. Zelie Martin

Parenting is a roller coaster of heartmelting moments and hair-pulling challenges. All while trying to raise kids to know God's love. For Christian parents, the goal is to guide your kids in their true identity - loved, chosen, and called to be saints.

St. Louis and St. Zélie Martin, parents of St. Thérèse of Lisieux, the Little Flower, embraced this principle. They have left us with five practical tips from their journey. These tips will help you raise children who shine in the Father's love, with a dose of grit and heart.

It's important to acknowledge that times have changed. Parenting in the 21st century comes with unique challenges that Sts. Louis and Zélie Martin never faced. Back then, there were no cell phones, Wi-Fi, or social media pulling at their kids' attention. These modern distractions make raising saints today feel like an uphill climb. However, God's grace is even more abundant to meet the moment. By leaning into that grace, you can adapt the Martins' timeless wisdom to navigate this digital screen age and guide your children toward holiness.

#1 Dedicate Each Child to God from the Start

Right after each birth, Zélie would pray, "Lord, grant me the grace that this child may be consecrated to You, and that nothing may tarnish the purity of its soul." From the beginning, she planted her children's lives in God's hands. She did not wait for them to reach the age of reason to start the saint-making process. It was a full upbringing in the Church from the start. You can do this too. Make sure to have your children baptized. Pray over your children often or have a family prayer routine before going to bed. Mark the child's forehead with the sign of the cross, using your thumb. This makes them feel loved, content, and blessed. This action says, "This child belongs to God."

#2 Love Your Children with Overflowing Amounts of Affection

Children need love like plants need water - tons of it, every day. Louis and Zélie knew this. Céline wrote about her dad, "Hard as he was on himself, he was always affectionate towards us.

His heart was exceptionally tender… No mother's heart could surpass his." Louis had a knack for nicknames. Marie was "the diamond," Pauline "the fine pearl," Céline "the dauntless one," Léonie "good-hearted," and Thérèse "the little queen" or "bouquet." Those names told each child, "You're special, and I see you." Go big with your love. Hug them, praise them, give them a nickname that lights up their soul. Make them feel like they're God's masterpiece, because they are.

#3 Don't Quit When Your Child's a Handful

Discipline and consistency is key to shaping character in children. The art of discipline lies in being firm, gentle, and consistent. Children should still feel the love they receive, even though you are clearly implementing rules and consequences, or when you are correcting a behavior that is not right. Some children come out swinging, and Zélie had her share. She wrote to her brother, "Do not be uneasy if you find your little Jeanne manifesting a temper… I remember how Pauline, up to the age of two, was the same, and now she is my best." Thérèse and Léonie gave her plenty of headaches too, but Zélie refused to throw in the towel. She set firm boundaries with love, knowing tough phases are not what define a child's future. When your child's tantrums or attitude make you want to hide, dig in.

Stay consistent, love fiercely, and trust that God's working in them, even when it feels like you're herding cats.

#4 Live the Faith You Want Them to Follow

Children are comparable to human lie detectors. They see through our nonsense and mimic what we do. Céline remembered a time Louis dealt with a rude tenant: "The woman refused to pay and ran after him crying insulting things. I was horrified, but he remained calm and made no reply." That quiet strength wasn't just for show. It taught his daughters how to love like Christ. Do you want your children to be kind, patient, and forgiving? Live it first. Your actions are the loudest sermon they will ever hear, so make it a good one.

#5 Get Down and Play Like It's Your Job

In a world where screens are the easy babysitter, Louis and Zélie remind us that play is where connection happens. Zélie played with her daughters, even if it meant burning the midnight oil to finish her work. Céline said, "She even willingly played with us, at the risk of having her own day's work prolonged to midnight or after." Louis was right there too, making toys, inventing games, and singing with them. For them, play was love in action. It showed their children that they were worth every minute. Ditch the devices, get on the floor, and build a fort or sing a silly song. Those moments tell your children, "You're my priority, and God's joy lives in you."

Louis and Zélie Martin did not have a parenting manual, but they had faith, grit, and a whole lot of love. Their tips aren't about perfection. They are about showing up, day after day, to raise children who know they are embraced by the Father. So, take a page from their book, and parent like you're raising saints. Because you are.

Activities to Grow in God's Gifts

1. **Family Gratitude Jar:** Create a family gratitude jar. Each day, have everyone write down one thing they're thankful for and place it in the jar. At the end of the week, read the notes together and thank God for His gifts.
2. **Body and Soul Game:** Play a game with your child where you name different experiences (e.g., feeling happy, being tired, loving someone) and ask if it's the body or soul. This helps children understand their identity as both body and soul.
3. **A Puffin's Prayer:** Help your child draw or craft a puffin (like Puffel!) If you have the stuffed Puffel plushie, display it as a reminder of God's love. Say a prayer with your child before going to bed, having them thank God for one gift they are thankful for.
4. **Empathy in Action:** Encourage your child to do one kind act for a friend or family member, like sharing a toy or writing a kind note. Discuss how it made the other person feel.

A Note from the Author

In the beginning of Christ's public ministry, we read that *a voice came from the heavens, saying, "This is my beloved Son, with whom I am well pleased" (Mt 3:17).* When God glorified his only Son, he revealed Christ's identity as "beloved." When we rise from the waters of Baptism, our Heavenly Father also proclaims, "This is my beloved son/daughter, with whom I am well pleased." From the beginning, our deepest identity is revealed - that you and I are beloved.

In writing *Puffel*, I didn't focus on a single child or a specific group. Instead, I drew inspiration from the diverse experiences of children across private, public, charter, and homeschool settings. Through conversations with young people, I recognized a universal longing for understanding, self-worth, and identity. These struggles demand urgent answers. Even apart from gender ideology, youth grapple with identity crises fueled by comparison and social anxiety as they navigate the complexities of growing up. We need to be concerned for all children because all children are *our* children. Like Tim Ballard says, they are "God's children." This understanding instills in us a deeper sense of responsibility. Our paternal and maternal instincts should extend beyond the confines of our own households. A good parent embraces all children as their own. My prayer for every child is to realize their deepest identity - that they are perfectly lovable in the eyes of the Father. My prayer for each reader of this book is that you may protect the precious dignity of each child in your life - fiercely, faithfully, and fruitfully.

You're never too young to learn about the gift of who you are and who you are called to be.

Through a Parent's Eyes

"Trust your instincts; you know your baby better than anyone else. Don't be afraid to ask for help, whether it's from family, friends, or professionals. When they say "it all comes to you naturally" believe them, because over time it really does. Remember that a "new you" was also born, so give yourself time to adjust and get to know yourself & your new life. It's okay to feel overwhelmed."

Samra, Mom of Newborn Baby

"As a father of five young children, I've come to understand that parents must take ownership in forming their children on the matters that are crucial to salvation; particularly faith, love, and sexuality. Don't rely solely on schools and churches. Seek out resources that can help you educate your children in the home in age-appropriate ways. There are plenty of effective ones out there."

David, Father of 5 Children

"Being a father has been among the most rewarding, scary, and beautiful adventures I've ever undertaken. Any success I've ever found in parenting has come directly from my participation in the life of the Church, which has given me the grace to model God's fatherhood in a way that has made up for my personal limitations. The more I accepted my shortcomings as a parent and asked God for help, the more He seemed to transform my inadequacies into self-confidence to be a better father."

Mike, Father of 2 Grown Daughters

References

Assor, A., & Tal, K. (2012). When parents' affection depends on child's achievement: Parental conditional positive regard, self-aggrandizement, shame and coping in adolescents. *Journal of adolescence*, *35*(2), 249-260.

Catholic Church. (1994). *Catechism of the Catholic Church.* Libreria Editrice Vaticana.

Hughes, D. A., & Baylin, J. (2012). *Brain-based parenting: The neuroscience of caregiving for healthy attachment.* WW Norton & Company.

Neufeld, G., & Maté, G. (2019). Hold on to your kids: Why parents need to matter more than peers (Updated ed.). Vintage Canada.

Perry, B. D., & Szalavitz, M. (2017). *The boy who was raised as a dog: And other stories from a child psychiatrist's notebook--What traumatized children can teach us about loss, love, and healing.* Hachette UK.

www.ingramcontent.com/pod-product-compliance
Lightning Source LLC
La Vergne TN
LVHW040221110826
845146LV00005B/1371

* 9 7 9 8 8 8 8 7 0 5 4 6 9 *